KANJI
STARTER 2

KANJI

STARTER 2

by
Daiki Kusuya

IBC Publishing

Published by IBC Publishing, Inc.
Ryoshu Kagurazaka Bldg. 9F, 29-3 Nakazato-cho
Shinjuku-ku, Tokyo 162-0804, Japan
www.ibcpub.co.jp

Printed in Korea.

ISBN978-4-925080-83-5

PREFACE

This book follows the same principle as in the previous book, "Kanji Starter"—utilizing pictographs and integrating characters in order to more easily recognize kanji characters.

The pictographs or ideas explaining kanji characters in this book may not necessarily be based on their historical development. They may be alterations or even my own creations. Again, the purpose of this book is to know the meanings of kanji characters, not to study how they were derived.

CONTENTS

SECTION 1

Excerpt from "Kanji Starter"

The following Kanji characters are explained in the previous book, "Kanji Starter." These are cited here for the purpose of explaining kanji characters newly appearing in this book.

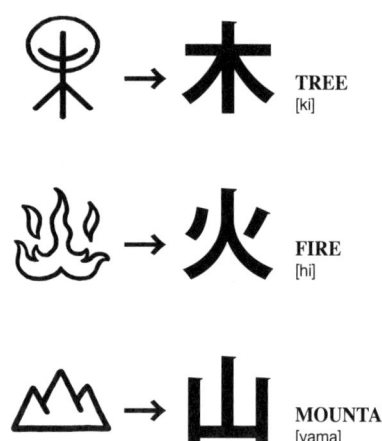

木 TREE [ki]

火 FIRE [hi]

山 MOUNTAIN [yama]

 **VALLEY**
[tani]

area between
mountains

 **STONE**
[ishi]

cliff and a piece

 **WATER**
[mizu]

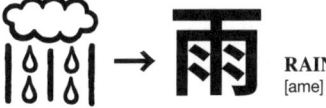 **RAIN**
[ame]

☼ → ⊙ → 日 **SUN,
DAY**
[hi]

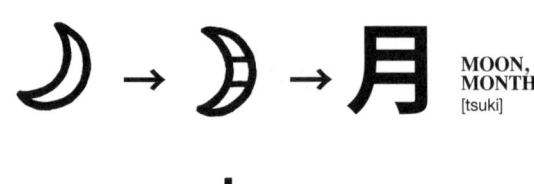

MOON, MONTH
[tsuki]

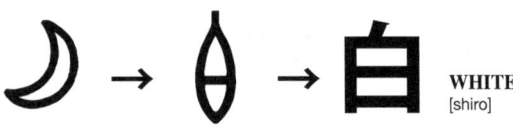

WHITE
[shiro]

shining moon

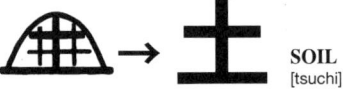

SOIL
[tsuchi]

mound

GOLD, MONEY
[kin]

a mountain, soil and nuggets

PERSON
[hito]

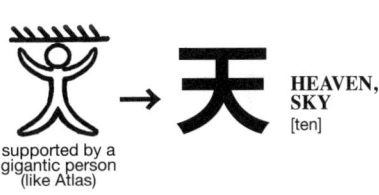 **HEAVEN, SKY** [ten]

supported by a gigantic person (like Atlas)

 **SMALL** [chī-sai]　**LITTLE, LESS** [suku-nai]

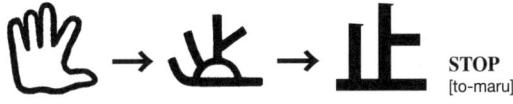 **STOP** [to-maru]

 **ENGINEERING** [kō]

 **GATE** [mon]

 **DOOR**
[to]

 **COW**
[ushi]

 **SHEEP**
[hitsuji]

→ 馬 **HORSE**
[uma]

→ 羽 **WING, FEATHER**
[hane]

12

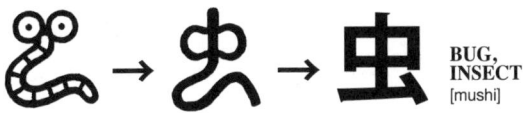 **BUG, INSECT** [mushi]

 **SHELL** [kai]

⬤→目 **EYE** [me]

→見 **LOOK, WATCH** [mi-ru]

→耳 **EAR** [mimi]

13

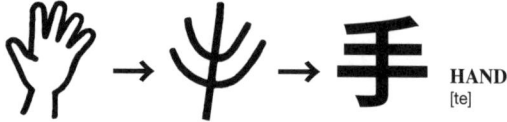 **HAND** [te]

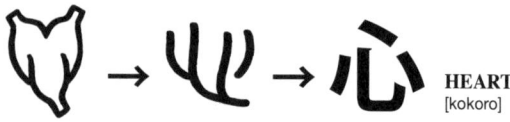 **HEART** [kokoro]

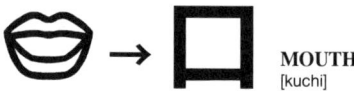 **MOUTH** [kuchi]

 **SAY, TELL** [i-u]

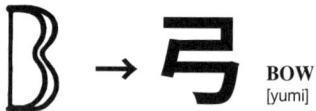 **BOW** [yumi]

 WHEEL, CAR [kuruma]

 BAMBOO [take]

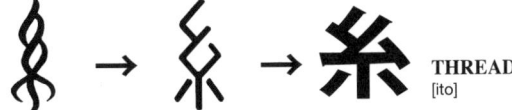 THREAD [ito]

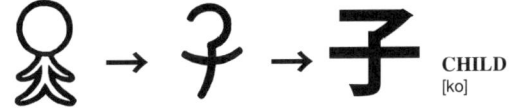 CHILD [ko]

relatively large head

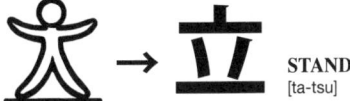 STAND [ta-tsu]

 **CROSS, EXCHANGE** [maji-waru]

a pregnant woman having large breasts

MOTHER [haha]

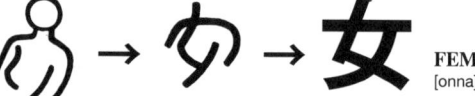 **FEMALE** [onna]

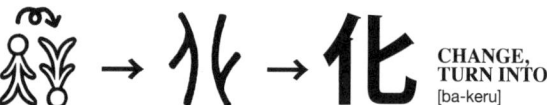

turn over

CHANGE, TURN INTO [ba-keru]

wind and snow

WINTER [fuyu]

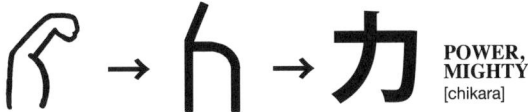

↗ → ↖ → **力**   **POWER, MIGHTY**
[chikara]

∫ → **刀**   **SWORD**
[katana]

⌐ → **斤**   **HATCHET, AX**
[kin]

古 → **古**   **OLD**
[furu-i]

ancient crown

囨 → **固**   **FIRM, SOLD**
[kata-i]

outer surface of
an old thing

One kanji character may be pronounced in different ways depending on how it is used. In SECTION 1 and SECTION 2, only one or two possible ways to pronounce the character are shown along with each character.

Numerals refer to the page on which the character was introduced.

stump

**ORIGIN,
BASIS**
[moto]

a fingerprint for
identity

**IDENTICAL,
THE SAME**
[ona-ji]

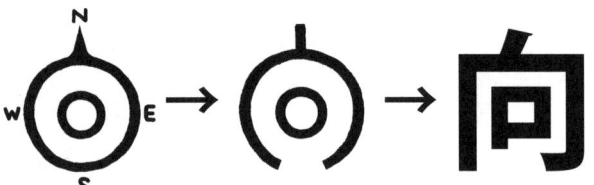

compass

**DIRECTION,
POINT TOWARD**
[mu-ku]

**CIRCLE, YEN
(Japanese currency)**
[en]

左 → 左

LEFT
[hidari]

右 → 右

RIGHT
[migi]

hit the wall,
cannot go farther

**UN-, DIS-
(makes negative
words)**
[fu]

11

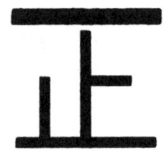 

stop a car exactly at
the line

**RIGHT,
CORRECT,
PROPER**
[tada-shii]

 →

a house with a long
corridor

**WIDE, LARGE
(in terms of space)**
[hiro-i]

**LEAVE,
GO AWAY**
[sa-ru]

23

soapbox

**STAGE,
A STAND**
[dai]

**COMBINE,
FIT**
[a-u]

 →

a table in a room

MEET
[a-u]

an eye checking time

NOW
[ima]

 →

a spike making a ...

HOLE
[ana]

① bull's-eye

② something *falls into* a category

HIT, FALL ON
[a-teru]
**THIS,
THE VERY**
[tou]

12

N.Z., in the "south,"
is famous for
sheep

SOUTH
[minami]

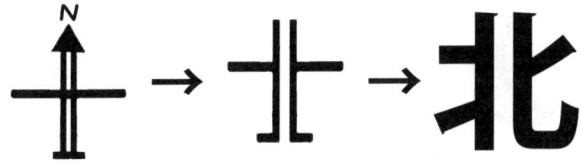

on the corner of
a map

NORTH
[kita]

head of an animal

**BEFORE,
FRONT**
[mae]

the moon and the door

OUTSIDE
[soto]

 →

something glittering
deep in a tunnel

DEEP INSIDE
[oku]

 早

the **sun** rising above
the horizon

EARLY
[haya-i]

9

the **sun** comes
up over the
horizon

RISE
[nobo-ru]

FLY
[to-bu]

 → 朝

9, 10

sun rises between
grass (=horizon) while
moon is almost gone

MORNING
[asa]

a person
watching the
moon from house

NIGHT
[yoru]

31

11

use two hands
on the **gate**

OPEN
[a-keru]

11

a hand and a bar

CLOSE
[shi-meru]

閞 → 閞 → 関

11

① mechanism to close a **gate** has closely connected parts

② the **gate** opens only for a person who has passed inspection

CONCERNED WITH, CLOSELY RELATED
[kaka-waru]

GATEWAY, CHECKPOINT
[kan]

互 → 互

two hooks

TO EACH OTHER, RECIPROCAL
[taga-i]

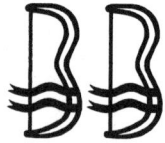 

14

a decorated **bow** for
a ceremony, not for
practical use

WEAK
[yowa-i]

silk string (from silk
worm) on a **bow**

13,14

STRONG
[tsuyo-i]

11

a person sent from
heaven to the earth

KING
[ou]

the **king** under a roof
completely rules all

**ALL,
COMPLETE**
[sube-te]

① the **king** is at the center of everything

② the **main** person in a group

MAIN
[omo-na]
MASTER
[shu]

in ancient times, the
king was the only
person who owned
precious gems or pearls

**BALL,
PRECIOUS THING**
[tama]

precious things
inside a border

COUNTRY
[kuni]

a mat on which a
person can lie

**BASED ON,
CAUSE**
[yo-ru]

the bridegroom puts
his hair up with a pin
in an ancient wedding

HUSBAND
[otto]

a **husband** was hit by
his wife with a bat and
fell unconscious

**LOSE,
MISS**
[ushina-u]

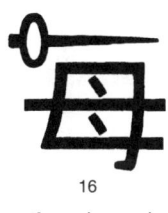 →

16

mother pins up her
hair "every" day

EVERY
[mai]

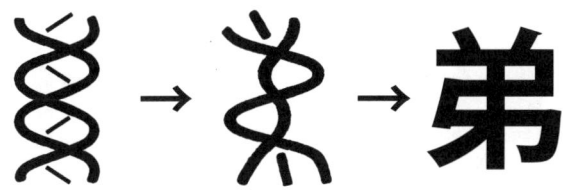

family genes

**YOUNGER
BROTHER**
[otouto]

 →

samurai warrior

**OFFICER,
WARRIOR**
[shi]

 →

two persons
side by side

COMPARE
[kura-beru]

a person crouching
down, covered with a
blanket

WRAP
[tsutsu-mu]

a person beside a sake
container, serving sake

DISTRIBUTE
[kuba-ru]

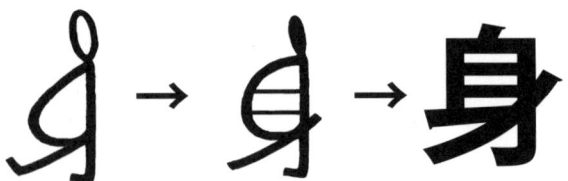

BODY
[mi]

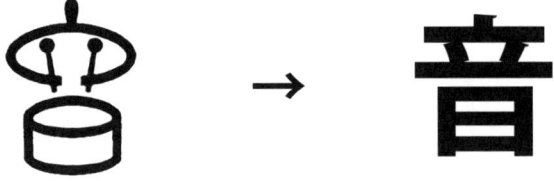

SOUND
[oto]

 →

easygoing juggler

**FUN,
EASY**
[raku]

a person with a "full"
stomach

**FULL,
FILL**
[jū]

育 → 育 → 育

a baby on a bed

**BRING UP,
REAR**
[soda-teru]

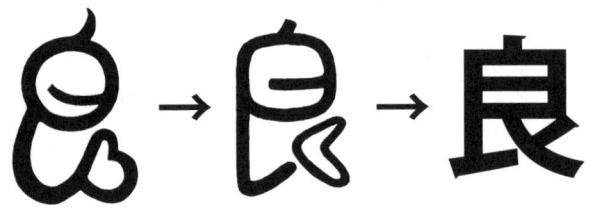

良 → 良 → 良

thumbs-up

GOOD
[yo-i]

 →

something **good** like
cake in a mouth

EAT
[ta-beru]

 →

in ancient times,
people used their
fingers to **eat**

**MEAL,
COOKED RICE**
[meshi]

 →

a person with his
mouth open → there is
a space

LACK
[ka-keru]

 →

① an officer calling…

② sequence

NEXT
[tsugi]

**(mathematical)
ORDER**
[ji]

**SHOUT,
SCREAM**
[sake-bu]

put an X mark on the
dead person's chest
for protection from bad
spirits

**EVIL,
BAD LUCK**
[kyou]

a pattern on the
chest → letters

**TEXT,
SENTENCE
(as in writing)**
[bun]

SUPPORT
[sasa-eru]

 →

15

threadlike lines
between skull plates

THIN, SLIM
[hoso-i]
MINUTE, FINE
[koma-kai]

 →

14

in your mind and in
your **heart**

THINK OF
[omo-u]

 →

in Japan, pointing to
one's nose indicates
"myself"

**SELF,
SPONTANEOUS**
[mizuka-ra]

 →

BAD SMELL
[nio-u]

 →

wrinkly face

GROW OLD
[o-iru]

a wise old man with a
beard contemplating

THINK
[kanga-eru]

NUMBERS

ONE
[ichi]

TWO
[ni]

THREE
[san]

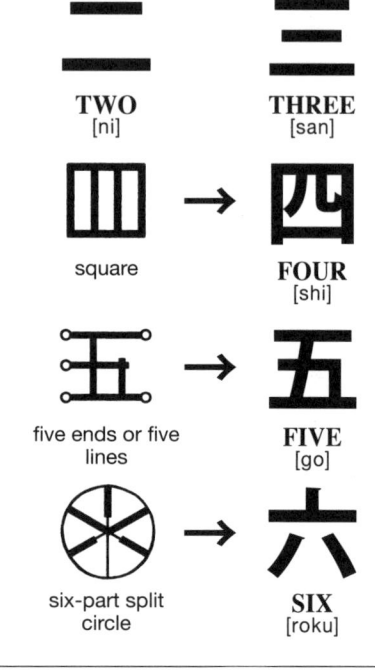

square

→ **FOUR**
[shi]

five ends or five
lines

→ **FIVE**
[go]

six-part split
circle

→ **SIX**
[roku]

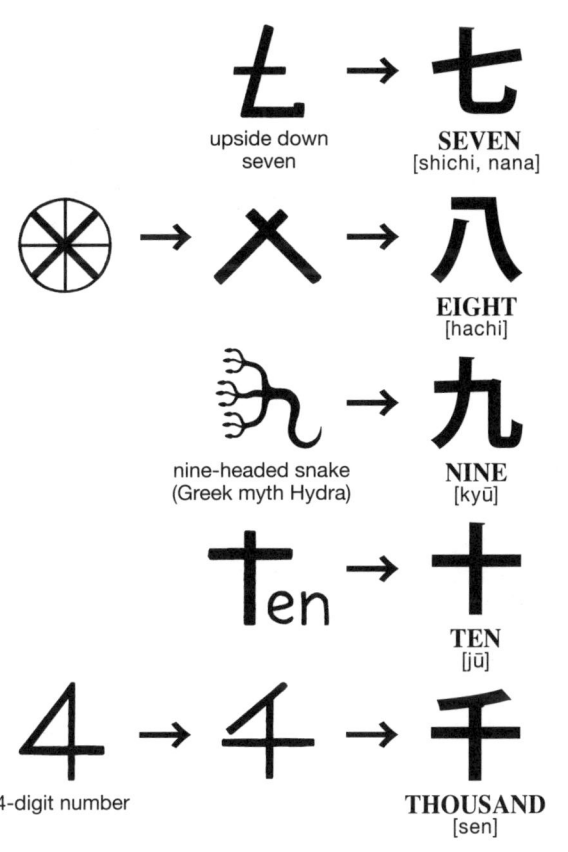

七 upside down seven → **SEVEN** [shichi, nana] 七

⊕ → ✕ → **EIGHT** [hachi] 八

nine-headed snake (Greek myth Hydra) → **NINE** [kyū] 九

✝en → **TEN** [jū] 十

4 4-digit number → ✝ → **THOUSAND** [sen] 千

**BEAN,
PEA**
[mame]

streaky bacon

**MEAT,
FLESH**
[niku]

**WHEAT,
BARLEY**
[mugi]

the fibers of a thread

**ELEMENT,
ORIGINAL,
PLAIN**
[moto]

 →

15

a **thread** is connected
to another thread

SOMETHING
RELATED,
SYSTEM,
LINEAGE
[kei]

a watermelon
sliced open

FRUIT,
ESSENCE,
SUBSTANTIAL
[mi]

56

HORN
[tsuno]
CORNER
[kado]

**SHELL (of turtle),
BACK OF THE HAND**
[kou]

FANG
[kiba]

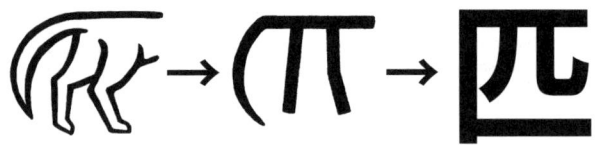

**a counter for
animals**
[hiki, piki, biki]

 →

16

young leafy plant later
changes into...

FLOWER
[hana]

flower arrangement

ART
[gei]

 → 菌

a smelly colony in a
petri dish

**GERM,
FUNGUS**
[kin]

branch of a tree

**GENERATION,
GENERAL PUBLIC,
WORLD**
[se, yo]

8

a **tree** with many
branches

→

LEAF
[ha]

① flag indicating that "market" is open

② area that grows around the **market**

MARKET
[ichi]
CITY
[shi]

TOWN
(administrative)
[machi]

many streets

CITY
(a hectic area/street)
[machi]

 →

separated areas by
borders

**DISTRICT,
WARD**
[ku]

 →

building with a bell
hanging inside

TEMPLE
[tera]

63

place where one can
relax

**HOUSE,
HOME**
[ie]

building with shelf and
display case

**SHOP,
STORE**
[mise]

64

SEAT
[seki]

12

a **horse** is hitched to
a post

STATION
[eki]

 → 富

a house with a big
container full of rice

**RICH,
WEALTH**
[tomi]

**CLOTHES,
DRESS**
[koromo]

**HANG,
SUSPEND**
[tsuru-su]

atomizer

**FRAGRANCE,
SCENT**
[kao-ri]

67

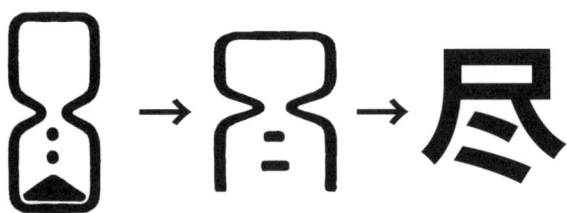

hourglass

**USED UP,
RUN OUT**
[tsu-kiru]

scales

**MEASURE,
PLOT**
[haka-ru]

 →

weight of piled books

HEAVY
[omo-i]
HEAP UP
[kasa-neru]

books on a shelf

VOLUME
[satsu]

 →

① displayed cans

② the value of an **article**

**GOODS,
ARTICLE**
[shina]

QUALITY
[hin]

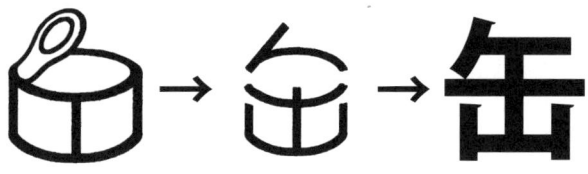

a container with
a pop-top

CAN
[kan]

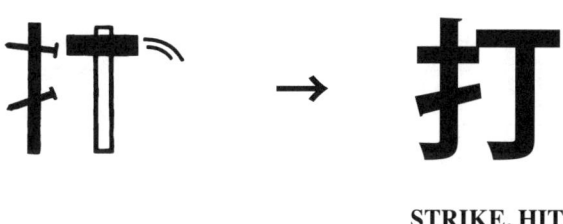

STRIKE, HIT
[u-tsu]

13

knife used to open a
clam

**MEANS FOR WORK,
IMPLEMENT**
[gu]

attaché case

→

**COMMERCE,
DO BUSINESS**
[akina-u]

① a frame

② a design

**PICTURE,
DRAWING**
[ga]

DRAW UP A PLAN
[kaku]

 →

**IGNITE,
POINT, DOT**
[tsu-keru]

 →

**SHINE,
ILLUMINATE**
[te-rasu]

COLORS

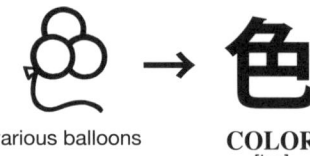

various balloons

COLOR
[iro]

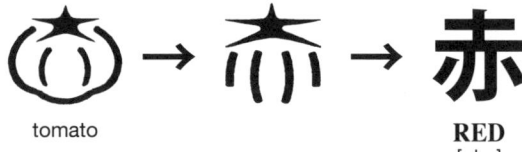

tomato

RED
[aka]

hydrangea

PURPLE
[murasaki]

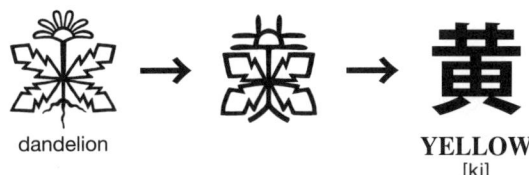

dandelion

YELLOW
[ki]

① color of soil
② **brown** beverage

BROWN [cha]
TEA [cha]

grasshopper

GREEN
[midori]

beyond the palm trees are the
blue sea and the blue sky

BLUE
[ao]

 →

10

a part of the plant that
pushes leaves up from the
ground like an arm does

**STEM,
STALK**
[kuki]

 →

15, 10

a **car** that can be lifted
up from the *ground* by
hand is…

LIGHT
[karu-i]

96

to hand something to
a **person**

→

**ADD,
GIVE**
[tu-keru]

a gem in the hand and
the house

→

PROTECT
[mamo-ru]

77

 →

14

hand holding a stick, chanting **mouth**
→ chief of the tribe who uses witchcraft

LORD (archaic),
YOU (contemporary)
[kimi]

 君

14

the first thing you
say when you meet
a person for the first
time

NAME
[na]

 →

in ancient times, a
warrior cut off his
enemy's ear (as proof
of his victory)

**TAKE,
GET**
[to-ru]

 → 反

a hand on the wall of
the prison pushing
against boundaries

**OPPOSE,
AGAINST**
[han]

 →

**CLOTH,
SPREAD**
[nuno]

 →

① uncommon **cloth**

② **rare**, hard to obtain

RARE
[mare]
HOPE
[ki]

something peeled
using a hand

**SKIN (noun),
HIDE (noun)**
[kawa]

hand to hand

**RECEIVE,
TAKE**
[u-keru]

81

 →

hand in hand

FRIEND
[tomo]

 →

97

hands surrounding a
friend (or simply, "4
hands")

**HELP,
SUPPORT**
[en]

82

 →

9

put a coat on a **friend's** shoulder to make the person "warm," like the **sun** does

WARM
[atata-kai]

 → 挙

14

RAISE TO SHOW, CITE
[a-geru]

**DEMON,
OGRE**
[oni]

ash/cinder under ground
(Japanese custom)

DEATH
[shi]

84

 →

death penalty

**CRIME,
GUILT**
[tsumi]

alien

**DIFFER,
FOREIGN**
[koto-naru]

a group of people
heading for the castle

SOLDIER
[hei]

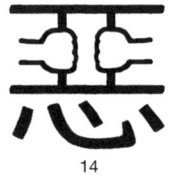

14

a villain in jail with evil
in his **heart**

BAD
[waru-i]

14

having something
strongly in one's **heart**

**ABSOLUTE,
WITHOUT FAIL**
[kanara-zu]

14

a hand grabs a
diamond someone
loves in a...

**HURRY,
URGENT**
[isogu]

14

state of **heart**
that makes angry
eyes

GET ANGRY
[oko-ru]

17

exerting great
force

**ENDEAVOR,
EFFORT**
[tsuto-meru]

 →

① view from the window

② there is nothing in the **sky**

SKY
[sora]

EMPTY
[kara]

migrating
birds stop by
mountains in the
ocean

ISLAND
[shima]

 →

rain and a turbine
make…

ELECTRIC
[den]

one form of **rain**
that looks like a
feather

SNOW
[yuki]

9

mass that brings
rain

CLOUD

[kumo]

energy
emanating from
the core

**GAS,
MOOD,
SPIRIT**

[ki]

boat, oar and
water

POND
[ike]

soil by **pond** → 地

10

**GROUND,
PLACE**
[chi]

SECTION 2

Boldface type in small letters indicates that the translation was introduced in SECTION 1 or immediately before.

Italic type indicates the extended translation, adapted from the original translation in SECTION 1.

Numerals refer to the page on which the character/ component was introduced.

COMPONENTS

(page 96–105)

Following are some components used in kanji characters. The meanings shown along with each component may not be the original (historical) ones and may have been altered somewhat so that the kanji character can be easily understood. They are not individual kanji characters and thus they do not have sound.

COMPONENTS

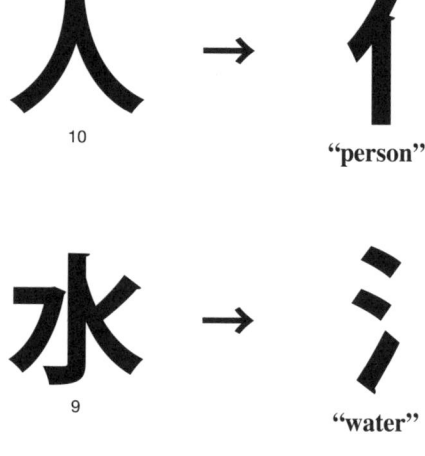

人
10
→ 亻
"person"

水
9
→ 氵
"water"

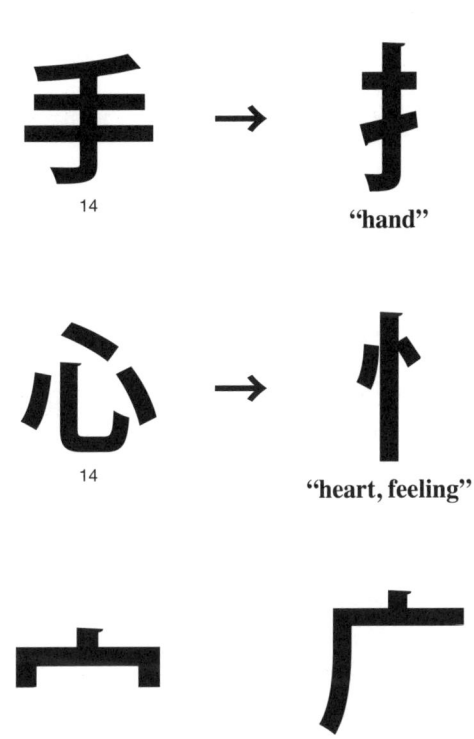

手 → 扌
14
"hand"

心 → 忄
14
"heart, feeling"

宀 → 广
"building, roof"

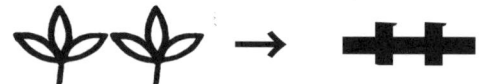

"plants"

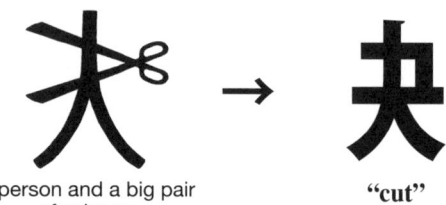

a person and a big pair
of scissors

"cut"

10

"moon" /
"meat, body part"
(the latter is derived from 肉→ p.54)

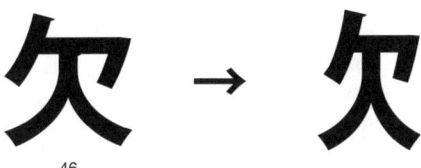

欠 → 欠

46

"lack, open,
open-mouthed"

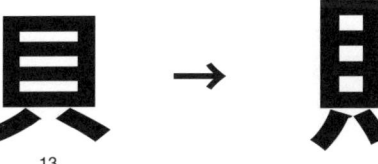

貝 → 貝

13

"shell, money,
valuable things"

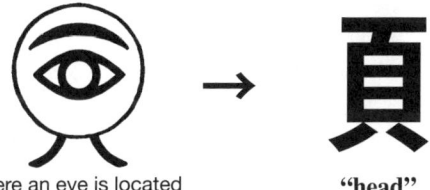

where an eye is located → 頁

"head"

 →

boxes stacked one on
top of another

"pile up"

 →

51

"old person"

 →

a hammer in a hand

"beat"

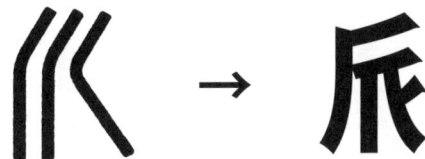

"stream that divides"

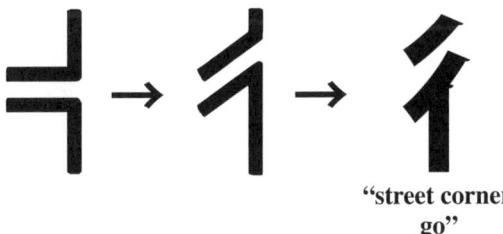

"street corner, go"

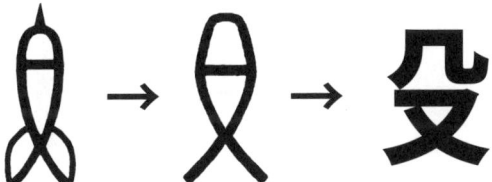

dart

"weapon for throwing, go far"

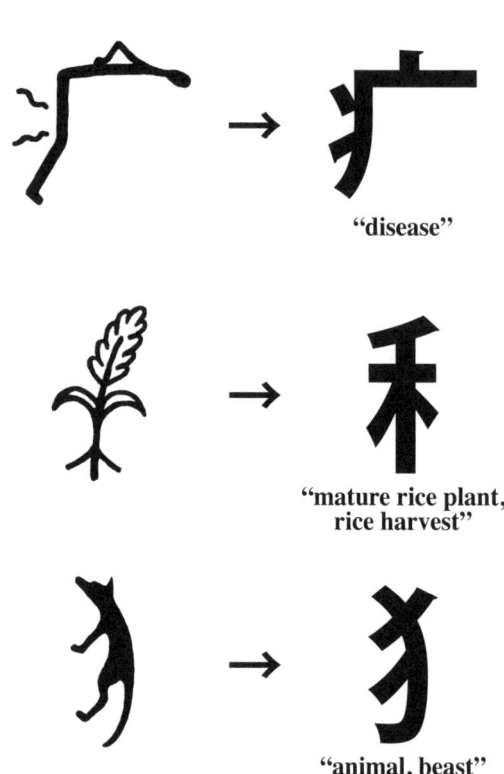

"disease"

"mature rice plant,
rice harvest"

"animal, beast"

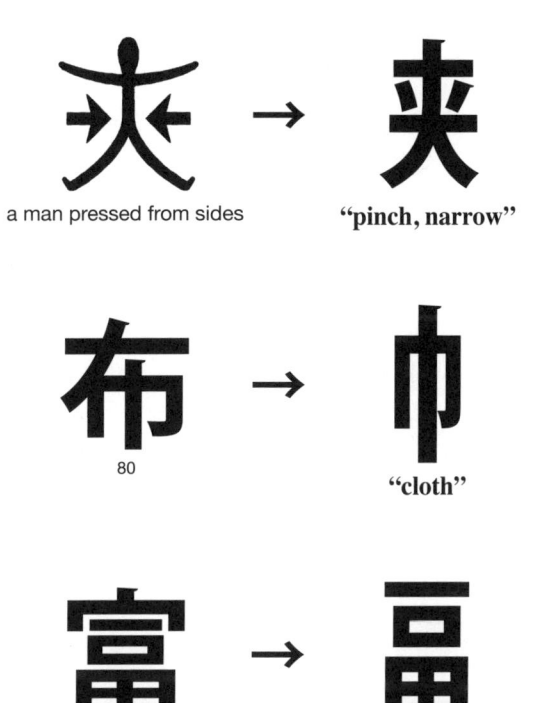

夾 → 夹

a man pressed from sides

"pinch, narrow"

布 → 巾

80

"cloth"

富 → 畐

66

"wealth"

 "sword"

 → 莫

① the sun setting between plants (=horizon), getting dark, the sun is…
② feel for something not seen (because **covered**)

"covered"
"look for"

① town square
② along the perimeter

"square"
"lap, cycle"

→ 辶
"street, road"

→ 隹
"bird"

gather and arrange books → 侖
"in order"

97   19

the **foundation** of a **house** should be...

**PERFECT,
COMPLETE,
FINISH**
[kan]

97   15

a **child** in a **house** is not playing but
writing...

**LETTERS (as
those in words)**
[ji]

97   16

① when a **woman** is there, **home** is...

② a **woman** tries to manage the *family* budget

SAFE
[an]

CHEAP
[yasu-i]

广 97 + 木 8 → 床

the **wood** under a **roof**

FLOOR
[yuka]

广 97 + 人 10 + 人 + 土 10 → 座

people on the *ground* under the **roof**

**SIT,
SEAT**
[suwa-ru]

金 10 + 同 19 → 銅

looks *similar* to **gold**

COPPER
[dou]

竹 + 同 → 筒

a hollow cylinder *just like* **bamboo**

TUBE
[tsutsu]

不 + 口 → 否

**DENIAL,
SAY NO**
[hi]

口 + 土 → 吐

from the **mouth** to the *ground*

**PUSH OUT FROM
MOUTH (SPIT,
VOMIT, EXHALE)**
[ha-ku]

the *words* are **right**

**PROOF,
EVIDENCE**
[akashi]

a **hand** *rolls out* pizza dough

**SPREAD,
ENLARGE**
[kaku]

search for **gold** in a **big** space

MINING
[kou]

水 + 台 → 治

96 ・ 24

water behind a *dam*

GOVERN
[osa-meru],
RECOVER
[nao-ru]

女 + 台 → 始

16 ・ 24

a **woman** on a **stage** will "begin" to sing

BEGIN
[haji-meru]

手 + 穴 + 木 → 探

97 ・ 26 ・ 8

with your **hand** in a **hole** in a **tree**

SEARCH
[saga-su]

水 + 穴 + 木 → 深

96　　　26　　　8

the **water** in the **hole** in the **tree** is…

DEEP
[fuka-i]

水 + 夜 → 液

96　　　31

dew forms at **night**

LIQUID
[eki]

⺌⺌ + 早 → 草

98　　　29

early stage of **plant** (without a flower)

GRASS
[kusa]

herbal formula to regain health and *happy feeling*

MEDICINE
[kusuri]

① tea made from **old herbs** tastes…

② and to drink it all is…

BITTER
[niga-i]
PAINFUL
[kuru-shii]

the **person** has a **solidly** established character

**INDIVIDUAL,
a counter for
small things**
[ko]

112

木 + 主 → 柱

8   36

the **main** piece of **wood** that holds up the roof

PILLAR, POST
[hashira]

人 + 主 → 住

96   36

the **main** place a **person** stays is their home

LIVE IN
[su-mu]

水 + 毎 → 海

96   39

water is *everywhere*

SEA
[umi]

心 + 毎 → 悔

97   39

a **feeling** that one has **every** time
after a mistake

REGRET
[kuya-mu]

心 + 夬 → 快

97   98

the **feeling** when all your worries
are **cut** away

**PLEASANT,
FINE**
[kokoroyo-i]

水 + 夬 → 決

96   98

sweating while "deciding" which wire to
cut to defuse the bomb

DECIDE
[ki-meru]

比
40

+

白
10

→

皆

**ALL,
EVERYONE**
[mina]

when you **compare white** things, all are
the same color

羽
12

+

白
10

→

習

**PRACTICE,
LEARN**
[nara-u]

quill pen and **blank** paper for studying

音
42

+

心
14

→

意

**WILL,
MIND**
[i]

sound (words) from the **heart**

115

土 + 音 + 人 → 境
10   42   10

① the *land* limit where *citizens* can go or *speak* freely

② the **border** is fixed under certain conditions

BORDER
[sakai]

SITUATION
[kyou]

金 + 音 + 人 → 鏡
10   42   10

metal that can reflect **sound** or **human** figure

MIRROR
[kagami]

金 + 充 → 銃
10   43

loading *metal* balls into a...

GUN
[jū]

金 + 良 → 銀

10   44

the next **best** *metal* to gold

SILVER
[gin]

女 + 良 → 娘

16   44

DAUGHTER,
GIRL
[musume]

羊 + 食 → 養

12   45

raise a **sheep** for *food*

REAR,
FOSTER
[yashina-u]

117

食 + 包 → 飽

45   41

food **wrapped** in a stomach

**SATIATED,
SATURATED**
[a-kiru]

月 + 包 → 胞

98   41

biological **wrapping**

**MEMBRANE
SACK**
[hou]

手 + 包 → 抱

97   41

arms wrapping something

**HOLD
SOMETHING
IN ARMS,
EMBRACE**
[da-ku]

水 + 包 → 泡
96   41

water wrapping air

BUBBLE, FOAM
[awa]

石 + 包 → 砲
9   41

barrel in which a **stone** bullet is **wrapped** (held)

CANNON, GUN
[hou]

口 + 欠 → 吹
14   99

BLOW
[fu-ku]

火 + 欠 → 炊

8   99

blow on a **fire** to make the fire
bigger to…

COOK
[ta-ku]

食 + 欠 → 飲

45   99

eating without this **lacks** something

DRINK
[no-mu]

谷 + 欠 → 欲

9   99

a feeling of **lacking**, like a **valley** which
will never be filled

**DESIRE,
WANT**
[yoku]

水 + 谷 → 浴

96　　9

a clean *river* runs into a
valley and one wants to…

BATHE
[a-biru]

次 + 貝 → 資

46　　99

① the **next** project needs **money**

② something to be *based on*

FUNDS
[shi]

MATERIAL
[shi]

化 + 貝 → 貨

16　　99

① **sea shell exchangeable** for other
   things (in ancient times)

② things that can be bought with
   money

MONEY
[ka]

COMMODITY
[ka]

121

化 + 頁 → 傾

16   99

change the position of one's **head**

**TILT,
IMBALANCED**

[katamu-ku]

火 + 頁 → 煩

8   99

a *hot* **head** is…

**BOTHERSOME,
ANNOYING**

[wazura-washii]

貝 + 曾 → 贈

99   100

catch a **pile** of **clams** and give them to
someone

PRESENT

[oku-ru]

pile up some **soil**

INCREASE
[fu-eru]

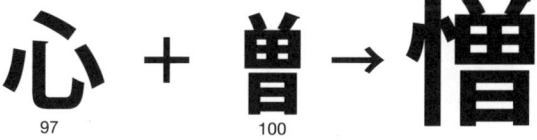

feeling that **piles up**

HATE
[niku-mu]

supportive (not main) part of a **tree**

BRANCH
[eda]

123

手 + 支 → 技

97   48

using **hands** to **support** one's career

**SKILL,
TECHNIQUE**
[waza]

月 + 支 → 肢

98   48

supportive part of the **body**

LIMB
[shi]

自 + 心 → 息

50   14

to make the **heart** beat and to keep
oneself alive

BREATH
[iki]

老 + 日 → 者

100   9

the nature of a human being is to get
older day by day

PERSON
[mono]

日 + 者 → 暑

9   125

a **person** under the **sun** feels…

HOT
(as in weather)
[atsu-i]

老 + 子 → 孝

100   15

the feeling of **children** for their *parents*

FILIAL PIETY
[kou]

孝 + 攵 → 教

125   100

a parent **spanks** a child to teach
him/her a *lesson*

TEACH
[oshi-eru]

貝 + 攵 → 敗

99   100

money lost through being **beaten**

**DEFEATED,
LOSE**
[yabu-reru]

正 + 攵 → 政

22   100

the **correct** use of *force*

POLITICS
[sei]

木 + 夂 → 枚
8   100

wood is **beaten** into pulp to make paper

**SHEET OF
(a counter)**
[mai]

牛 + 夂 → 牧
12   100

cows driven by **beating**

**STOCK FARM,
RAISE
LIVESTOCK**
[boku]

工 + 夂 → 攻
11   100

beat with *tools*

ATTACK
[se-meru]

127

エ + 力 → 功
11   17

engineering (tool) and **power**

ACHIEVEMENT
[kou]

月 + 厎 → 脈
98   101

dividing stream running in the **body**

(BLOOD)
STREAM,
PULSE
[myaku]

水 + 厎 → 派
96   101

water/things *separated from* the main
body

DERIVATIVE,
SECT
[ha]

人
96

+ 系
56

→ 係

the key **person** in a **system**

**A PERSON
IN CHARGE,
CONCERNED
WITH**
[kakari]

子
15

+ 系
56

→ 孫

child in a **lineage**

GRANDCHILD
[mago]

糸
15

+ 冬
16

→ 終

when icicles melt and become thin like
thread, the **winter** comes to an...

END
[o-waru]

角 + 虫 → 触

57   13

a **horn** is used by **insects**

TOUCH
[sawa-ru]

角 + 刀 + 牛 → 解

57   17   12

① *cut* **horns** off a **cow**

② **break up** and look at details to know things

BREAK UP, UNDO
[to-ku]
COMPREHEND
[kai]

手 + 甲 → 押

97   57

using your **hand** and seeing the **back of your hand** when you open a door

PUSH
[o-su]

女 + 市 → 姉

16　　61

female member of a family who goes to **market** often

ELDER SISTER
[ane]

馬 + 区 → 駆

12　　63

horses were used to communicate between **wards**

RUN, DRIVE SOMETHING INTO
[ka-keru]

日 + 寺 → 時

9　　63

during the **day** the **temple** bell rings to tell the …

TIME, HOUR
[toki, ji]

牛 + 寺 → 特
12　　　63

a **cow** offered to a **temple**

SPECIAL
[toku]

竹 + 寺 → 等
15　　　63

① **bamboo** used to make the fence of a **temple** all has the same length

② things are **equal** only in the same...

EQUAL
[hito-shii]

RANK
[tou]

言 + 寺 → 詩
14　　　63

(originally) *words* dedicated to God at a **temple**

POETRY
[shi]

人 + 寺 → 侍

96   63

a *guardian* of a **temple**

SAMURAI
[samurai]

彳 + 寺 → 待

101   63

everyone meets at the **temple**
on the **corner**

WAIT
[ma-tsu]
TO RECEIVE
A PERSON
[tai]

彳 + 殳 → 役

101   101

go with a **weapon** for military duty

DUTY,
ROLE
[yaku]

手 + 殳 → 投

97 101

a **hand** with a **weapon** will...

THROW
[na-geru]

水 + 殳 → 没

96 101

a **weapon** thrown into **water** will...

SINK
[botsu]

車 + 殳 + 手 → 撃

1 5 101 1 4

from a **car** a **weapon** is *thrown*

**ATTACK,
SHOOT**
[u-tsu]

疒 + 殳 → 疫

102 + 101

widely thrown (spread) **disease**

PLAGUE
[eki]

女 + 家 → 嫁

16 + 64

a **woman** joining a *family*

**BRIDE,
WIFE**
[yome]

人 + 衣 → 依

96 + 66

a **person** pulling another
person's *sleeve*

**RELY ON,
DEPENDENT
ON**
[yo-ru]

重 + 力 → 動

69　　17

a **heavy** thing has **power** applied to it

MOVE
[ugo-ku]

人 + 動 → 働

96　　136

a **person moving**

WORK
[hatara-ku]

禾 + 重 → 種

102　　69

① the head of a **rice plant** becomes **heavy** with…

② a group generated from the same **seed**, different from other groups

SEED
[tane]

KIND, SORT
[shu]

禾 + 家 → 稼

102   64

the **rice harvest** is the means by which
a *family* lives

EARN
[kase-gu]

禾 + 火 → 秋

102   8

season of **harvest** and **fire**-colored
leaves

AUTUMN
[aki]

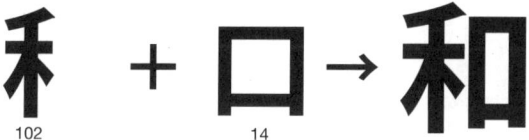

禾 + 口 → 和

102   14

harvested rice in the **mouth** gives one

**COMFORT,
HARMONY**
[nago-mu]

a *rice-stalk* hat on a **child**
(for a harvest festival)

SEASON
[ki]

tiny amount of **rice harvest**
→ tiny amount

**SECOND
(unit of time)**
[byou]

the best way to move if you need to
make *small* **stops**

WALK
[aru-ku]

木 + 交 → 校
8   16

a building with **crossed timbers**
→ a large wooden building

SCHOOL
[kou]

羽 + 異 → 翼
12   85

many **feathers** have a **different** function

WING
[tsubasa]

水 + 兵 → 浜
96   86

water brings **soldiers** to the…

**BEACH,
SHORE**
[hama]

君 + 羊 → 群

78 + 12

a **lord** who owns **sheep** has a herd of them

GROUP, HERD

[mure]

犭 + 守 → 狩

102 + 77

kill **beasts** to **protect** human lives

HUNT

[ka-ru]

犭 + 夹 → 狭

102 + 103

path made by **animals** *wedging* their ways through

NARROW

[sema-i]

手 + 夹 → 挟

97　　103

a **hand** making something **narrow**

PINCH
[hasa-mu]

山 + 夹 → 峡

8　　103

mountains pressing in on the sides

CANYON
[kyou]

布 + 日 + 目 → 帽

103　　9　　13

a thing made of **fabric** for protecting
eyes from the **sun**

HAT, CAP
[bou]

手 + 目 → 看

14   13

hands and **eyes** working on a thing

**LOOK
CAREFULLY,
LOOK AFTER**
[mi-ru]

103   103

a large **expensive** piece of **cloth**

WIDTH
[haba]

103   104

wealth *divided*

SUB-
[fuku]

莫 + 布 → 幕
104   103

cloth covering the stage

CURTAIN, SHROUD
[maku]

莫 + 力 → 募
104   17

look for powers

RECRUIT, COLLECT
[tsuno-ru]

莫 + 日 → 暮
104   9

① the **sun** is *gone*, the day is over

② spend days

COME TO AN END
[ku-reru]

TO LIVE
[ku-rasu]

月 + 莫 → 膜

98   104

a *biological* **covering** or film

MEMBRANE
[maku]

莫 + 土 → 墓

104   10

a dead body **covered** by **soil** is in a...

GRAVE, TOMB
[haka]

其 + 土 → 基

104   10

the foundation of a house is in a **square** hole in the **ground**

BASIS
[moto]

其 + 月 → 期
104   98

a lunar cycle

**PERIOD (of time),
TERM, STAGE**
[ki]

土 + 反 → 坂
10   79

to go up a *hill* you have to *fight* gravity

SLOPE
[saka]

木 + 反 → 板
8   79

against the natural form of the **tree**

BOARD
[ita]

money *comes and goes*

SALE
[han]

opposite way, way back

RETURN
[kae-ru]

an endless line of **cars** on a **highway**

CONTINUAL
[tsura-naru]

146

辶 + 隹 → 進
105   105

birds fly on a migratory **route**

**PROCEED,
ADVANCE**
[susu-mu]

辶 + 斤 → 近
105   17

cut a short **path** through the woods

**NEAR,
CLOSE**
[chika-i]

戸 + 斤 → 所
12   17

the proper "place" for a fire **ax** is behind
a glass **door**

PLACE
[tokoro]

147

立 + 木 + 斤 → 新

15   8   17

a **standing tree** is cut with an **ax** to make a "new" house

NEW
[atara-shii]

立 + 木 + 見 → 親

15   8   13

a person to be **looked** up to like a **standing tree**

PARENT
[oya]

INTIMATE
[shita-shii]

水 + 皮 → 波

96   81

the *surface* of the *sea*

WAVE
[nami]

石 + 皮 → 破

9   81

work on a **hide** with a **stone**

**TEAR,
BREAK**

[yabu-ru]

手 + 受 → 授

97   81

**GIVE,
GRANT**

[sazu-keru]

三 + 人 + 日 → 春

52   10   9

three people lying under the **sun**

**SPRING
(season)**

[haru]

七 + 刀 → 切

53   17

separate into **seven** pieces with a **sword**

CUT

[ki-ru]

九 + 木 + 隹 → 雑

53   8   105

in **nine trees**, various kinds of **birds** resting

MIS-CELLANEOUS

[zatsu]

水 + 九 + 木 → 染

96   53   8

use **nine** *liquids* obtained from **trees**

DYE

[so-meru]

石 + 九 + 十 → 砕

9   53   53

break a **stone** into **nine** or **ten** pieces

CRUSH
[kuda-ku]

十 + 具 → 真

53   71

something hidden that required **ten** *tools*
to reveal

**TRUTH,
GENUINE**
[shin]

水 + 青 → 清

96   75

the **blue** *sea* is...

CLEAN
[kiyo-i]

151

日 + 青 → 晴
9   75

sun and **blue** sky

**FINE
WEATHER**
[ha-re]

心 + 青 → 情
97   75

clear **heart**, *pure* **feeling**

**SYMPATHY,
EMOTION**
[jou]

言 + 青 → 請
14   75

talk to the **blue** sky (heaven)

REQUEST
[ko-u]

words in a carefully considered **order**

**ARGUE,
THEORY**
[ron-jiru]

people having *proper relations*

ETHICS
[rin]

ears revealing **feelings** (by turning red)

**EMBARRASS-
MENT,
SHAME**
[haji]

153

SECTION 3

idioms
COMBINATION
of two or more characters

元日 [ganjitsu]	(the **day** a year *starts*) ↓ **NEW YEAR'S DAY** 19, 9
同日 [doujitsu]	**(ON THE) SAME DAY** 19, 9
同一 [douitsu]	**SAMENESS, IDENTICALNESS** 19, 52
傾向 [keikou]	**TENDENCY** 122, 20
左手 [hidarite]	**LEFT HAND, ON THE LEFT** 21, 14

RIGHT HAND, ON THE RIGHT

[migite]

21, 14

ILLICITNESS, INJUSTICE

[fusei]

22, 22

NATIONAL DIET

[kokkai]

37, 25

TODAY

[kyou]

25, 9

THIS MONTH

[kongetsu]

25, 10

 **ON THAT DAY**

[toujitsu] 26, 9

 (**hit** the *point*)
↓
JUSTNESS, RIGHTEOUSNESS

[seitou] 22, 26

 **UNJUSTNESS, UNFAIRNESS**

[futou] 22, 26

 **ALTERNATE**

[kougo] 16, 33

 **PREVIOUS DAY, THE DAY BEFORE**

[zenjitsu] 28, 9

駅前 [ekimae]	**IN FRONT OF THE STATION** 65, 28
外車 [gaisha]	**IMPORTED CAR** 28, 15
外交 [gaikou]	**DIPLOMACY** 28, 16
今朝 [kesa]	**THIS MORNING** 25, 31
今夜 [kon-ya]	**TONIGHT** 25, 31

| 深夜 | LATE AT NIGHT, MIDNIGHT |
| [shin-ya] | 111, 31 |

| 関係 | RELATIONSHIP |
| [kankei] | 33, 129 |

| 関心 | INTEREST |
| [kanshin] | 33, 14 |

| 強弱 | STRONG AND WEAK |
| [kyoujaku] | 34, 34 |

| 強力 | POWERFUL, MIGHT |
| [kyouryoku] | 34, 17 |

安全 [anzen]	(no anxiety, **completely safe**) ↓ **SAFETY** 106, 35	
完全 [kanzen]	**PERFECT** 106, 35	
全力 [zenryoku]	**AT FULL POWER,** **WITH UTMOST EFFORT** 35, 17	
家主 [yanushi]	**LANDLORD** 64, 36	
国家 [kokka]	**NATION** 37, 64	

外国	**FOREIGN COUNTRY**
[gaikoku]	28, 37

外国人	**FOREIGNER**
[gaikokujin]	28, 37, 10

全国	**WHOLE COUNTRY**
[zenkoku]	35, 37

夫人	(the **person** with a **husband**) ↓ **WIFE**
[fujin]	38, 10

毎日	**EVERY DAY**
[mainichi]	39, 9

 **PARCEL**

[kozutsumi]   11, 41

 **ARRANGEMENT**

[tehai]   14, 41

 **WHOLE BODY**

[zenshin]   35, 42

 **ONESELF**

[jishin]   50, 42

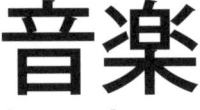 **MUSIC**

[ongaku]   42, 43

教育 [kyouiku]

EDUCATION

126, 44

不良 [furyou]

BADNESS, DELINQUENT

22, 44

良心 [ryoushin]

CONSCIENCE

44, 14

朝食 [choushoku]

BREAKFAST

31, 45

外食 [gaishoku]

EATING OUT

28, 45

一次 [ichiji]	**FIRST ORDER, PRIMARY** 52, 46
論文 [ronbun]	**THESIS** 153, 48
文化 [bunka]	(the result of the *developed* **writing**, i.e. knowledge) ↓ **CULTURE** 48, 16
思考 [shikou]	**THINKING** 49, 51
自立 [jiritsu]	**SELF-SUSTAINING, INDEPENDENCE** 50, 15

| 老人 | **OLD PERSON** |
| [roujin] | 51, 10 |

| 牛肉 | **BEEF** |
| [gyūniku] | 12, 54 |

| 皮肉 | (bitter comment that penetrates **skin** and reaches inside the **body**)
↓
IRONY |
| [hiniku] | 81, 54 |

| 小麦 | **WHEAT** |
| [komugi] | 11, 55 |

| 元素 | **ATOMIC ELEMENT** |
| [genso] | 19, 55 |

| 真実 | **TRUTH** |
| [shinjitsu] | 151, 56 |

| 実力 | **REAL ABILITY** |
| [jitsuryoku] | 56, 17 |

| 三角 | **TRIANGLE** |
| [sankaku] | 52, 57 |

| 花火 | **FIREWORKS** |
| [hanabi] | 59, 8 |

| 雑草 | **WEED** |
| [zassou] | 150, 111 |

| 海草 | **SEAWEED** |
| [kaisou] | 113, 111 |

| 投薬 | **ADMINISTERING A DRUG** |
| [touyaku] | 134, 112 |

| 文芸 | **LITERATURE** |
| [bungei] | 48, 59 |

| 細菌 | **GERM, BACTERIA** |
| [saikin] | 49, 60 |

| 市街地 | **URBAN DISTRICT** |
| [shigaichi] | 61, 62, 92 |

商店街 [shoutengai]	**SHOPPING STREET** 72, 64, 62
地区 [chiku]	**DISTRICT** 92, 63
音楽家 [ongakuka]	("music"+ a family business run at **home**) ↓ **MUSICIAN** 42, 43, 64
画家 [gaka]	**PAINTER** 72, 64
開店 [kaiten]	**OPENING A SHOP** 32, 64

支店 [shiten]	(a secondary **store** *away from the main* store) ↓ **BRANCH STORE** 48, 64
欠席 [kesseki]	**ABSENCE** 46, 65
座席 [zaseki]	**SEAT** 107, 65
空席 [kūseki]	**VACANT SEAT** 89, 65
香水 [kousui]	**PERFUME** 67, 9

 **CLOCK, WATCH**

[tokei]　　　131, 68

 **TOTAL**

[goukei]　　　24, 68

 **ACCOUNT, RECEIPT
(at restaurants)**

[kaikei]　　　25, 68

 **DOUBLE, OVERLAP**

[nijū]　　　52, 69

 **GRAVITY**

[jūryoku]　　　69, 17

 **COMMERCIAL GOODS, COMMODITIES**

[shouhin]

72, 70

 **FOOD PRODUCT**

[shokuhin]

45, 70

 **MEDICINE, A PHARMACEUTICAL**

[yakuhin]

112, 70

 **FURNITURE**

[kagu]

64, 71

 **STATIONERY**

[bungu]

48, 71

 (*area* separated by *line*)
↓
COMPARTMENT, ZONE

[kukaku]

63, 72

 **PLAN**

[keikaku]

68, 72

 **DEFECT**

[ketten]

46, 73

 **EMPHASIS, FOCUS**

[jūten]

69, 73

 **TERMINAL, LAST STOP**

[shūten]

129, 73

| 悪人 | **EVIL MAN, WICKED MAN** |
| [akunin] | 86, 10 |

| 悪化 | **GETTING WORSE** |
| [akka] | 86,16 |

| 悪口 | **BAD MOUTH, SPEAKING EVIL OF** |
| [warukuchi] | 86, 14 |

| 必見 | **MUST-SEE** |
| [hikken] | 87, 13 |

| 特急 | **LIMITED EXPRESS TRAIN** |
| [tokkyū] | 132, 87 |

努力
[doryoku]

ENDEAVOR

88, 17

真空
[shinkū]

VACUUM

151, 89

空手
[karate]

(martial art without using any
tools = "**empty hand**")
↓
KARATE

89, 14

空白
[kūhaku]

BLANK

89, 10

島国
[shimaguni]

ISLAND COUNTRY

89, 37

電池 [denchi]	(*stored* **electricity**) ↓ **BATTERY** 90, 92
充電 [jūden]	**ELECTRIC CHARGE** 43, 90
電力 [denryoku]	**ELECTRIC POWER** 90, 17
電車 [densha]	**TRAIN** 90, 15
電気 [denki]	**ELECTRICITY** 90, 91

空気 [kūki]	**AIR** 89, 91	
元気 [genki]	**HIGH SPIRIT, VITALITY** 19, 91	
正気 [shouki]	**CONSCIOUSNESS, SANITY** 22, 91	
人気 [ninki]	**POPULARITY** 10, 91	
天気 [tenki]	**WEATHER** 11, 91	

墓地	**CEMETERY**
[bochi]	144, 92

基地	**(MILITARY) BASE**
[kichi]	144, 92

土地	**LAND**
[tochi]	10, 92

見地	**VIEWPOINT**
[kenchi]	13, 92

名前	**NAME**
[namae]	78, 28

配布 [haifu]	**DISTRIBUTION** 41, 80	
友人 [yūjin]	**FRIEND** 82, 10	
親友 [shin-yū]	**CLOSE FRIEND** 148, 82	
支援 [shien]	**SUPPORT** 48, 82	
一気 [ikki]	**AT A BREATH, IN ONE GO** 52, 91	

 [ichiji]	**AT ONE POINT, TEMPORARILY, ONE O'CLOCK**	52, 131
 [shiki]	**FOUR SEASONS**	52, 138
 [tokushoku]	(**special color** that a thing has) ↓ **CHARACTERISTIC**	132, 74
 [moji]	**LETTER, CHARACTER**	48, 106
 [tenji]	**BRAILLE**	73, 106

赤字 [akaji]	**TO BE IN THE RED, DEFICIT** 74, 106
治安 [chian]	**PUBLIC PEACE, PUBLIC ORDER** 110, 106
安心 [anshin]	**PEACE OF MIND, RELIEF** 106, 14
不安 [fuan]	**ANXIETY** 22, 106
安否 [anpi]	**WHETHER ONE IS SAFE OR NOT** 106, 108

証人
[shounin]

WITNESS

109, 10

個人
[kojin]

INDIVIDUAL

112, 10

住人
[jūnin]

RESIDENT

113, 10

海外
[kaigai]

OVERSEAS

113, 28

海水浴
[kaisuiyoku]

SEA BATHING

113, 9, 121

不快 [fukai]	**UNPLEASANT** 22, 114
決心 [kesshin]	**DECISION,** **DETERMINATION** 114, 14
解決 [kaiketsu]	**SETTLEMENT, SOLUTION** 130, 114
決意 [ketsui]	**RESOLUTION** 114, 115
同意 [doui]	**CONSENT, AGREEMENT** 19, 115

意外 [igai]	*(better than or worse than your expectations)* ↓ **UNEXPECTED** 115, 28
国境 [kokkyou]	**COUNTRY BORDER** 37, 116
心境 [shinkyou]	**STATE OF HEART, STATE OF MIND** 14, 116
教養 [kyouyou]	**EDUCATION, SOPHISTICATION** 126, 117
細胞 [saibou]	**CELL** 49, 118

飲食店	**RESTAURANT**	
[inshokuten]		120, 45, 64
食欲	**APPETITE**	
[shokuyoku]		45, 120
投資	**INVESTMENT**	
[toushi]		134, 121
資金	**FUNDS**	
[shikin]		121, 10
金貨	**GOLD COIN**	
[kinka]		10, 121

雑貨 [zakka]	**MISCELLANEOUS GOODS**	150, 121
外貨 [gaika]	**FOREIGN CURRENCY**	28, 121
特技 [tokugi]	**PROFESSIONAL SKILL, SPECIAL SKILL**	132, 124
前者 [zensha]	**THE FORMER**	28, 125
敗者 [haisha]	**LOSER**	126, 125

役者	ACTOR, ACTRESS
[yakusha]	133, 125

教会	CHURCH
[kyoukai]	126, 25

教授	PROFESSOR
[kyouju]	126, 149

失敗	FAILURE
[shippai]	38, 126

政治	POLITICS
[seiji]	126, 110

山脈 [sanmyaku]	(a range of **mountains** runs like a *vein*) ↓ **MOUNTAIN RANGE** 8, 128
文脈 [bunmyaku]	**CONTEXT** 48, 128
子孫 [shison]	**OFFSPRING** 15, 129
終電 [shūden]	**LAST TRAIN** 129, 90
開始 [kaishi]	**TO BEGIN** 32, 110

正解 [seikai]	(**correct comprehension** of the question) ↓ **CORRECT ANSWER** 22, 130
同時 [douji]	**AT THE SAME TIME** 19, 131
一等 [ittou]	**FIRST CLASS,** **FIRST ORDER** 52, 132
期待 [kitai]	(**waiting** for the *time* when a thing is realized) ↓ **EXPECTATION** 145, 133
役所 [yakusho]	**GOVERNMENT OFFICE** 133, 147

主役 [shuyaku]	**LEADING ROLE** 36, 133	
攻撃 [kougeki]	**ATTACK** 127, 134	
自動 [jidou]	**AUTOMATIC** 50, 136	
自動車 [jidousha]	**AUTOMOBILE** 50, 136, 15	
手動 [shudou]	**MANUAL OPERATION** 14, 136	

一種 [isshu]	**A KIND OF** 52, 136	
人種 [jinshu]	**HUMAN RACE** 10, 136	
種子 [shushi]	**SEED** 136, 15	
進歩 [shinpo]	**ADVANCEMENT, PROGRESS** 147 138	
全校 [zenkou]	**THE WHOLE SCHOOL** 35, 139	

字幕 [jimaku]	**SUBTITLE** 106, 143	
募金 [bokin]	**FUND-RAISE** 143, 10	
基金 [kikin]	**FUNDS** 144, 10	
前期 [zenki]	**FIRST TERM, PREVIOUS TERM** 28, 145	
早期 [souki]	**EARLY STAGE** 29, 145	

思春期 PUBERTY

[shishunki]　　49, 149, 145

期日 DUE DATE, DEADLINE

[kijitsu]　　145, 9

近所 NEIGHBORHOOD

[kinjyo]　　147, 147

住所 ADDRESS

[jūsho]　　113, 147

台所 (**place** with a *counter* to serve)
↓
KITCHEN

[daidokoro]　　24, 147

新車 [shinsha]	**BRAND-NEW CAR** 148, 15
青春 [seishun]	**YOUTH, SPRINGTIME OF LIFE** 75, 149
親切 [shinsetsu]	(*gentleness* that *penetrates*) ↓ **KINDNESS** 148, 150
同情 [doujou]	**SYMPATHY** 19, 152
友情 [yūjou]	**FRIENDSHIP** 82, 152

 **PUBLIC OPINION**

[seron]

 **QUARREL**

[kouron]

INDEX

In this index, the characters are arranged simply by the number of lines in the character, not by the number of real strokes. For example, 口 (mouth) is categorized in "4 lines" in this index, but it is written with 3 strokes in proper orthography.

202

❏ **12 LINES** ❏

❏ **13 LINES** ❏

BIBLIOGRAPHY

Shinjigen 232nd edition. Kadokawashoten, 1985, Tokyo

Jōyōjikai. Shizuka Shirakawa, Heibonsha, 2003, Tokyo

The Kodansha Kanji Learner's Dictionary. Jack Halpern, Kodansha International Ltd., 1999, Tokyo

KANJI STARTER 2

2004 年 10 月 25 日　第 1 刷発行
2012 年 12 月 25 日　第 8 刷発行

著　者　**楠谷 大樹**

発行者　**浦　晋亮**

発行所　**IBC パブリッシング株式会社**
　　　　〒 162-0804 東京都新宿区中里町 29 番 3 号
　　　　菱秀神楽坂ビル 9F
　　　　Tel. 03-3513-4511　Fax. 03-3513-4512
　　　　www.ibcpub.co.jp

印刷所　Chong-A Printing co.

ISBN978-4-925080-83-5